No Way Out

No Way Out
(In Chicago)

Amir Humphries

authorHOUSE®

AuthorHouse™
1663 Liberty Drive
Bloomington, IN 47403
www.authorhouse.com
Phone: 1-800-839-8640

Published by AuthorHouse 8/13/2012

ISBN: 978-1-4670-5179-8 (sc)
ISBN: 978-1-4670-5171-2 (sc)

Library of Congress Control Number: 2011918432

Epigraph Quote

"Rock On"

Author Notes
(The Reason for the Book)

There are too many kids killing kids. The youth of today has little or no guidance, loyalty, or respect. This message is to inspire the youth on their decision making, and influence young men to grow and become real men. If you have made a mistake in your life, its never too late to turn it around which can lead to a prosperous future.

Dedication

I dedicate this to my mom who has been the back-bone for me and my three brothers. My mom has been through a lot and with God in her life, has turned her life around and has made some good decisions. She has turned out to be a fantastic wife, grandmother, aunt, and super mom.

Acknowledgement

Frist I want to thank God for all the blessings I have been blessed with. Thanks to all the people that He has brought into my life so that I can give the youth a thought of a way out. Thanks to my Mom and Dad, I love you guys. Thanks to Tony Dwalton for showing my Mom a different way of life. I also would like to thank my wife Trecia Humphries, because if it wasn't for her there is no telling how my life would have turned out. I would like to thank my four kids Devonte, Amir Jr., Ashante, Denigah, who give me inspiration to live and keep fighting everyday. I would like to give a special thanks to Erik Manuel for inspiring me to make the ending an inspiring one for the youth of today, and another special thanks for all that I have come in contact with. Through my walk in this life I want to thank Faye Wiseman, who during the course of me growing up took me out of the hood and showed me a different side of life and God. To all my Aunts and Uncles who have gone before me, and all my cousins, I love you all with all my heart.

Wearing an orange jumpsuit with 201833 across my back, I started telling my story. "What a difference a day makes," I began …

From down the hall, I heard my name being called.

"Baraka," Mookie yelled, "get your tail up!"

With a grunt, I said, "Gone somewhere My cousin Mookie slapped me on the head and ran down the hall yelling, "Grandma! You better tell that high-yellow girl to quit playing so much!"

I heard Mookie go into the kitchen and ask Grandma what she was cooking. "It smells really good," she said.

"Grits, bacon, eggs, and homemade biscuits," Grandma replied.

There was a knock on the door, and Mookie yelled, "Who is it?"

"It's Art."

"Who?" Mookie asked again.

"It's Art!"

Mookie turned and yelled, "Baraka, your smelly friend Art is at the door."

I walked down the hall to the door and opened it. "What's up, joe, I'll be out in a minute," I said, then turned to my grandma. "Did my mother called last night?"

"No, baby, but I'm sure she'll be by here later on today."

I grabbed my coat, and Grandma yelled, "Boy, where are you going? You didn't touch your breakfast!"

"But they're waiting on me," I said as I gave her a kiss. "I love you, Grandma."

"I love you too. Be safe in those streets."

"What's up, joe—did you hear all that noise last night?" I asked Art once we were outside.

"Yeah, it sounded like the Fourth of July. It sounded like they were shooting for about an hour, man," Art said.

"Quit blowing stuff out of proportion," I teased him.

"No—it did seem like about an hour. Anyway, did ya'll finish ya'll homework?"

"Nah," I said, "cause I was with your mama last night."

"Baraka—what kind of name is that? Sounds like something you catch on your feet."

We were still laughing as we entered the school. The day went by as usual—until recess when all the kids gathered around to play a game called Johnny Come Across. When I tried to make my way to the other side, I ran headfirst into a brick wall, and all the kids laughed. I went to the nurse's office, and my uncle was called to the school to pick me up. When word got around school, my friends thought I got into a fight and went home early.

Around 2:45, there was a knock on the door. Grandma answered the door, and the kids there said, "Mrs. Humphries, can we speak to Baraka?"

I went to the door, and one of my friends said, "Damn, man! What happened? We thought you got jumped."

"Nah, man, we were at recess playing Johnny Come Across and I ran into a wall—that's how I got this hickie. I'm all right, man. I know you guys love me, I'll holla at you all later."

Later on that day, my mom, Helen, came home.

"Mom, I need to talk to you," I said. "There's this girl that likes me; her name is Jackie. She wrote me a love letter using the words from a song, and there's a house party this Saturday."

My mom looked at me and said, "Boy, do you even know how to dance?"

"I'm a gangster, Mom!"

"Okay, gangster, let me see what you got." Laughing hard, my mom called her mother into the room and said, "Momma, come check your grandbaby out!"

Grandma came in the room and said, "Go ahead, baby, get your boogie on."

"Momma, you need to stop," said Helen. She looked at me and said, "Boy, let me show you a few tricks of the trade."

"Hey, Ms. Brown, how you doing?" I said to Art's mom the next day when I went to pick him up.

"Fine. What's going on, Baraka?"

"Nothing much. My mom said to tell you hi." Turning to Art, I said, "Art, you ready?"

Art replied, "Let's roll."

After we left, I said, "Man, did you see what Jackie had on today? Yo! She was looking so good."

"You should have seen Melisa. Man, I told her she

was looking good, and she smiled, said thanks, and kissed me on the cheek. Man, I damn near fainted."

We both laughed as we entered the park. I yelled out, "Who got next?" to a bunch of kids playing basketball, and then we teamed up and the game went on.

After the game, as we walked home, I said, "Man, you couldn't stop me today.

"You couldn't stop me either," Art said.

When we returned to the building where we stayed, we put the hoop up and played until Mookie yelled out, "Baraka, it's time to bring your tail in the house!"

Art turned to me and said, "You got lucky this time, but you know it's not over."

We were so competitive; everything was a battle. We would pitch pennies, play Trouble, strike' em out, and a winner had to be declared. If not, the game would go on until it was clear who won. Art was my best friend; what I didn't have, Art had—and the other way around. Art was the best dancer in the neighborhood, which got us into parties for free; that was Art's specialty.

When we were twelve, my mom took us on our first trip out of Chicago; we went to Florida. I was having a ball, but Art seemed a little distant. I asked him if he was all right, and Art said, "This is real nice of you and your mom, but it would have been nice to have my mom here."

"It's cool," I said, "but it's a big difference from all the shooting every night, the drugs, smelly hallways, and the gangs."

"You know what? You're right," Art agreed. "Last one to the other side of the pool is a rotten egg."

"Man, you know I can't swim!"

"Me neither," Art said.

The day we returned to Chicago, it was zero degrees with a wind chill of negative two.

A week later, Art, Lashaun, Kenny, Terrence, and I tried out for the basketball team; we were told the results would be out Friday. When the list was posted, to our surprise, none of our names were on the list.

When I got home and told my mom, she said, "So, honey, were you that bad? Or were the other guys that good?"

"Neither one," I said.

On Monday, my mom called the school, and that's when she was told that sixth graders couldn't join the team. Mrs. McGuire said she would check into it to find out why. Before the school day ended, Kenny and I were called to the gym by Mr. Johnson, who told us we made the team. We were pretty sure it was because of our height, because the only time we got into a game was when our team was winning by fifteen or more points. We finished the season 10–6 and made it to the second round of the playoffs.

School was out, and the summer began; everybody was out. Fire hydrants were wide open, snow cones were being sold, little kids were on the swings, house music was blasting, and cars were driving by with their booming systems.

The king of black disciples made his way to the park and pulled up in a Chevy Blazer with two cars leading the way and three cars in back. He got out of the truck, and everyone showed him love by throwing up gang sign. He had "next" on the basketball court, and everyone gathered around to see the big boys play ball.

By mid-summer, my friends and I were all on summer basketball teams. My team played against Art's team for the championship, and we won by six points. I had fifteen points, fifteen rebounds, and was voted MVP of the tournament. Art was named Co-MVP, and if his team had won, he would have been MVP.

By the end of the summer, Art had moved to

the south side but still attended St. Callistus with me. He and I made the school basketball team and were stars in our positions. In seventh grade, our team was 1–15 for the season, and the following year, we were 14–2 and then lost the championship to Resurrection by three points.

During the season, we became closer friends. We would go downtown to Mr. Subs, Dunkin Donuts, and the three-dollar dollar movie before one o'clock.

Close to graduation, Dushay was having a graduation party. Art came over with a couple of friends from his new neighborhood—the type of guys who stole cars, sold drugs, and robbed whoever they came in contact with who wasn't on their level. We were in the hallway drinking a bottle of Old English 800 when one of the guys pulled out a joint. I said, "Art, what's up? You smoke now?"

He said, "Baraka, this is what I do. But don't worry, if you get high, I got your back."

We left the building and headed over to the party. It seemed as if everyone had been waiting on us to get there, because when we walked in, everyone gave us daps and represented. We partied, and then shots rang out—one of my boys got shot in the stomach. He died on the way to the hospital.

We later found out that it was our rival gang that had come through shooting. The Disciples were in an uproar that night and out for revenge, which cut Art's visit short—and the guys he came with.

June 15, 1986. It was graduation day from the 8th grade. I stood there with my shiny grey suit and burgundy tie, while Art wore burgundy pants, a white shirt, and a grey tie. In all my years in school, I was never called for the Honor Roll, but this time I made the list. As they called "Baraka Humphries," my family cheered for joy. That was an exciting time for us; we took pictures, laughed, and enjoyed the moment.

Needless to say, Art and I partied that night, and by now you know how we partied. Art and some of his guys came and scooped me up in a sweet car. I asked Art, "Whose car is this?"

Lil Mike looked at Art and said, "Is this guy serious?" Then he said, "Look at the steering wheel—don't you see the collar is missing?" But it was graduation night, so it didn't matter. We just rode around and kept drinking, smoking, and hitting that powder. By 12:30, we had run out of everything, including money, so one of the guys said, "Let's find us a victim and get our paper right."

A feeling came over me, so I said, "Take me to the crib."

"Baraka, what's up?" Art said.

"Man, take me to the crib now."

Three days passed and I hadn't heard from Art. I went to his crib and knocked on his door. I said hey to his mom and asked her how she was doing. "Not too good," she said. I asked what was wrong, and she stood silently for a minute and then said, "Art is in jail."

I asked what happened, and she said, "They got him for armed robbery and for being an occupant in a stolen vehicle. Baraka, baby, get your mind right because there's nothing out here in these streets."

So I was gonna use this summer to get my mind right. Little did I know that my best friend was going to receive four years and I was going to learn about my mom's extracurricular activities.

"Mom!" I yelled. I opened the bedroom door and witnessed the crack pipe fall from her mouth.

"What the hell! You come in my room and didn't knock on the door."

"Momma, I'm sorry, but you didn't say anything when I called your name."

The next morning, she sat me down and we had a long talk. Let's just say from there, my whole thought process changed. I never knew—I guess I just didn't want to believe it—that my mother is a crack head. That didn't change the way I felt; I loved her with mind, body, and soul.

Mookie yelled, "Baraka! Grandma said get in this house." So I gave my boys some dap, threw up our gang sign, and headed to the house.

While I was waiting for the elevator, Curtis walked by and said, "What's up, Lil Rock and gave me some dap."

I looked at him and said, "Man, my name is Baraka."

"I know, but when you smoke weed like I do, who can say that name? You can ball, so I'm going to call you Lil Rock."

"I can roll with that," I said.

Curtis was signaled by "KD" to come around the corner. As I was waiting at the elevator, I heard them arguing. KD said, "Who are you talking to like that?" As the elevator opened and I started towards it, I heard a bang, followed by two more—bang, bang. I looked to the right and saw Curtis's body drop, his head wide open. I looked in his eyes as he twitched, then stared at KD with a sharp, piercing look as his gun fell to his side and the elevator door closed. I couldn't believe I was just talking to Curtis three minutes ago. My hands and body were shaking.

I made it upstairs, and Grandma asked, "What's wrong, baby?"

"Nothing, Grandma."

An hour and forty-five minutes later, there was a knock at the door.

"Who is it?" my grandmother said.

"Detective Jackson and Whitter." They were better known as Action 'n' Jackson. "We'd like to speak to your grandson about a murder that took place an hour and a half ago."

"Well what does my grandson have to do with it?"

"The elevator camera shows him looking to the right as he stepped into the elevator. We have a few suspects in custody, and we want to know if he can identify them."

They took me to the station, and in custody were KD, KD's right-hand man Skillet, Bo-leg, and Roni. "Son, can you identify the shooter?" they asked me.

"Like I told you all before, all I saw was the body drop and no shooter."

The police interrogated KD and his gang then let them go.

After that, something had changed. It seemed as if everyone was looking at me funny. I didn't know if it was because I didn't tell or if I should have told, but I was getting a lot of respect from the older gang members.

One day, as the sun was fading, I was shooting ball in the park. Three cars pulled up, a door opened, and a voice said, "Little homey, come here." As I approached, I saw it was KD. I was looking him straight in the eyes. I stood by the door, and as he got out of the car, he asked, "Do you know who I am? Everyone knows who you are." He pulled his gun from his waist and said, "Are you scared?"

As I stuck my gun to his waist, I said, "Of what? My dad taught me to fear no man, that you bleed like I do—or maybe even more."

"Get in and let's take a ride," he said.

"My mom told me not to ride with strangers," I said with a smirk.

"You're funny too. Get your little ass in."

Everything was quiet at first in the car, then he asked, "Do you smoke?"

"Weed," I said.

He told me that when you're high, it clouds your judgment and your reaction time, and in these streets you have to have an advantage. "What was your conversation with the police?" he asked.

"With all respect, I'm trying to forget the whole thing, and you know I didn't tell them anything because this little ride wouldn't be happening."

"For a young buck, you're kinda loose at the lips."

"My dad told me to always look a man in the eyes, and if you're speaking the truth, a real man can't do nothing but respect that."

He just looked at me and shook his head.

We road around just kicking it until it was time for me to go home. He pulled up to the building and handed me a knot. I told him, "I'm cool."

Insisting I take the money, he said, "I don't want you to ever feel like you owe me something, therefore I won't feel like I owe you something. Tomorrow, after you do your homework—you do do your homework, don't you?—page me and I'll be by to pick you up."

It seemed like I had the whole world in my hands. We rolled and talked every day. I had earned the respect of everyone in the hood and on every side of town. Not only because I rode with him, but also because I started on his basketball team. I was only thirteen, 6'3" and 150 pounds and was killing them.

He took me under his wing and showed me a lot of things, especially the dope game.

We hit the tables one night, and I had never seen so many drugs in my life—not even on TV. We were in and then we were out. It was always business at the table, but everyone had fun, and after everything got divided, everyone was happy. He made sure everyone stayed on their P's and Q's but kept everyone happy and treated everyone fairly. At the same time, he was a maniac if you crossed him.

He told me to always get your folks on one page and always believe in your system. "If I'm making five thousand and you're making two thousand, we all are eating good. Always have a code for when you're being set up. The person who takes the hit will be taken care of while he's in and will be blessed when he gets out. You have to give them a sense of security and loyalty, therefore you can stay in the game a long time and make a lot of money. Never send a man on a mission that you wouldn't go on yourself. I'm around every day; I keep my ears to the ground so I can hear them coming and keep my eyes open so I can know where to go."

I had to be the luckiest guy in the world. I was making over 40,000 a week and was about to start varsity as a freshmen. I was a 6'3" small forward with a silky smooth point guard that went by the name of Silk, a 5'11" shooting guard by the name of Judon, a 6'4" 200-pound power forward by the name of Chris, and a 6'5" center with curls. They were juniors and were ranked in the top twenty-five in the nation.

The first game of the season in the house was wall to wall. I scored twenty-six points, had fifteen rebounds, and made eight assists. Homecoming was approaching—the day after my birthday—and we were hosting the number-two team in the nation. I had forty points, twenty rebounds, and ten assists. The final score was 101–75. The homecoming party was that night, and we were ready to party.

That was the first time I danced with her. She was so beautiful that night, captain of the cheerleader team and the prettiest thing I had ever seen. "I've been looking for you," I said to her.

"For what?" Rhonda said.

"So I can tell you how pretty you look."

By then, a group of guys bum rushed me and were singing happy birthday. Then a slow song came on, and she told one of her friends, "Girl, let me find my baby." She turned and saw me and said, "There he is."

We grew really close after that night. If I wasn't over at her house, then she was over at mine. I had never thought for one minute that my life could be like this. I had become a basketball sensation and was feared by everyone who knew who I hung with. You can call it loved by many and feared by plenty. It seemed as if the world was mine.

We finished the season 28–0 as state champions and the number-one team in the nation.

Throughout the season, the gang violence had been growing out of control. The news was always talking about someone getting shot or someone getting killed. I often missed my guy—my right-hand man Art. I wondered how he was doing. I kept money on his books but refused to go see him in that cage after my first and only visit. We talked for hours that first visit, and he told me about how rough it was for him and his mindset. I told him what was going on with me, how I was having the best of both worlds. He had become a big-time gang leader of the Vice Lords from the opposite side. That didn't matter to me. He was still my dog even though I was moving up in the ranks of the Black Disciples.

School was out and summer had rolled around again. As usual, everyone was out on the streets.

KD pulled up, followed by three more cars. They approached me, and he said, "I need you to ride with me tonight."

I said, "No problem, but what's up?"

"Something's going down and I need you there."

I didn't know what I was getting into, but since it was KD, it didn't matter.

We pulled up to an all-night car wash, followed by two more cars. As we were about to go through, a guy got in our car. We exchanged packages as we rode through the car wash. We had just scored a hundred pounds of cocaine and were heading to the hideout.

We pulled up like normal, and the two other people in the car got out with KD. The two stood by the door while I kept the car going. About five minutes passed and I had to urinate really bad. I got out the car and went behind the building. As I came from behind the building, I noticed the two guys were gone, so I took another way back to the car. I saw that one of the guys was waiting on me to return to the car. I crept up behind him, placed my gun to his head, and asked what was going on. I said, "Speak now or hold your breath cause I'm going in anyway."

We walked up to the door, and then I stood to the side. He knocked on the door, and the dude asked, "Is the door clear?"

"Yeah," he said.

When he opened the door, I shot him and made the other dude back his way back into the house. As I entered the house, there were two other guys strapped to chairs and shot in the head.

"Where is he?" I asked.

"Upstairs," the dude said. I shot him twice and moved on up the stairs.

I took a deep breath going up the stairs. A door was open, and I could hear KD yelling, "You punk MF! I'm not telling you shit!"

The guy yells, "Bring the alcohol upstairs! I'm gonna show your ass." He didn't get a response, so he yelled again and started toward the stairs. I snuck behind him and shot him in the head, then caught his body and dragged it back into the room. As his body dropped, I could see KD covered in blood from head to toe and Meisha sitting beside him smoking a cigarette. KD looked at her and said, "You're a dirty ole bitch."

"I had nothing to do with it," she said.

KD looked at me and said, "Kill da bitch. She set me up."

I unloaded the clip on her, and then he told me where the safe was and the combo.

"Come on, KD," I said. "I'm gonna get you out of here."

"It's too late," he said. "I love you like a son; you have the power to lead, change lives, and do something with your life before the streets take it away from you."

I looked at him with tears in my eyes because I knew they would be the last words I would hear him say. I grabbed the briefcase out of the safe and started moving. I got in the car and put my hand over my face trying to figure out what just happened. I knew my life was about to change. I had two million in cash and over a hundred kilos of drugs.

A week later, I buried KD. After the funeral, I met with all the gang members to find out who ordered the hit. We were shaking up every side of town, but no one would talk. So for the rest of the summer, everyone was on edge.

Usually for Labor Day, before we would return to school, KD would have a basketball tournament, softball games, and a huge cookout just to celebrate us returning to school. The winning teams would get school supplies, backpacks, and jackets; all the other participants would get school supplies. So to continue his legacy, I hosted this year's cookout, keeping everything as KD did back then.

It was show time again; basketball season was about to start and I was the number-one sophomore in the nation. During an interview, the reporter asked me, "Baraka, why do you bring your whole team to your interviews?"

"Let me ask you a question," I said. "How can you tell if a star is truly shining?"

The reporter said, "That's a good question."

"Surround yourself with other stars—like my teammates—and that makes me shine."

The reporter said, "That's right. You've got to love this guy."

We won the state championship again that year.

Two years later, as a senior on the basketball circuit, there wasn't a college out there that wasn't trying to get me to play for them, but on the street circuit, every cop wanted to link me to gang activity. They hauled in some of my top dogs and even some of the senior citizens from the block, but no one would talk. Everyone knew that if they were loyal, they would be taken care of if something were to happen. If they needed to be bailed out, I had their back, or if they had to do time, I always made sure they had money on the books. They also knew that if they crossed me, I would seek revenge, and if I couldn't get you, I would get the person next to you.

It was the end of May. I was graduating, and my best friend was getting out of jail. I had plenty of money, was a basketball star, and had more power than I ever imagined I would. I was picking up Art three weeks before my graduation in a pearl white Maxima. As he came out, he had a cold stone look, but as soon as he saw me, he broke a cold hard smile.

We kicked it all day, just talking and eating and trying to make up for lost time. I told him we were going to a party, but in reality I was giving him a surprise party. He was really surprised because I had a room full of chicks. It seemed as if we were having a good time until he passed me a joint.

He looked at me and in an angry voice said, "What the fuck you mean, you don't smoke anymore? Man, we're celebrating me coming home."

"I know that, man, but I still don't smoke."

"So you mean to tell me you too good to smoke with your homeboy?"

I hugged his shoulder and said, "Man, let me talk to you. Listen, if you weren't who you are, I would have put a bullet in you. Do me a favor—don't ever disrespect me again, especially in front of my folks."

Art said, "Homeboy, you forgot who the fuck I am. I just did four years in the pen, and you gonna have the nerves to tell me to watch my mouth."

I looked at him. Art smiled and said, "Oh is that supposed to scare me? Man, my bad. I'm tripping it—the weed and the Hennessey. You know I love you and don't mean no disrespect."

We hung out for about two weeks, day and night, night and day. Then one day, I told Art I needed to talk to him. "I just found out some good news, and I have some decisions to make," I said. "Trice is two weeks pregnant, and I made a decision to go to the University of Illinois."

Art said, "Man, I just got out, and you're about to go? You gonna leave all you got here—all that money and power—to go to college?"

I just smiled and said, "Not my money, man. And knowledge is power. KD once told me that the most dangerous man is a man that has both street and book knowledge, like our forty-fourth president would be. I'm about to have a baby, and it's no longer about me. I have to make it about my seed."

Graduation had to be one of the happiest days of my life—walking across the stage to receive my diploma, and the sounds of all that cheering. My press conference was to be held in three weeks to see if I would attend college or go to the pros; I chose to further my education.

Later that summer, I had a cookout because I had to report to college three weeks before school started. It was a good day for me and my family because I was the first child to attend college that was from the inner city. The park was packed, and everyone was having fun playing basketball, eating, and just hanging out. Four carloads of guys pulled up, and Art got out; he was drunk and high, and so where the guys he was with.

I greeted him as they got out of the car. "What's up, man?"

"Nothing," he said. "Just wanted to see my boy off before he left."

"Man, let me holla at you for a minute. You know them cats can't be in this neighborhood!"

Art said, "Man, why you tripping?"

"What the fuck do you mean? This is your second time disrespecting me in front of my guys."

"Man, I just came by to holla and be on my way."

"You just take care of yourself, Art," I said. "Ever since you got out, you been acting different.

"So have you," he said.

"Well I leave at six, so if you can, come by and holla before I leave."

School was going great, basketball season was starting, and we were ranked the number-one team in the nation. I was averaging twenty-eight points, seven assists, and twelve rebounds. I was on ESPN all the time.

One Thursday, after playing Duke, I received a phone call from my mother, saying that Trice got robbed and was in the hospital. I told her I was on the way. I asked if the baby was okay, and she said yes and that Trice was fine too—that she was more scared than anything else. "You don't need to come home, son. Just stay there and stay focused. We'll take care of her and the baby."

"But Ma …" I started to say.

"Baby, have I ever let you down?

"No, Mom. I love you. Make sure she calls me."

"I got you. And I love you too."

Trice and I talked a lot on the phone for the next several months and things went back to normal.

It was the week of the Final Four—what a great week. I lead my team to the championship game that would be played in four days.

My phone rang. "Hello? Hello? Baraka?" she said.

"Mom?"

"They done shoot my baby—my baby, they shot him. I want you home right now. NOW!"

I got to the hospital four hours later and was greeted by Shawn and my old gang. "Where's my mom?" I asked.

"She's in room 1627."

When I got to the room, I walked in and said, "Hey, Mom?"

She stood up and held me real hard. I looked over at my brother who was in the hospital bed and said, "Hey, little homey?"

He squeezed my hand and said, "Did ya'll win?"

"Yes we did."

He smirked and said, "You know I'm gonna be better than you."

I looked at him and said, "I know, little brother."

"I love you."

"I love you too," I said. He squeezed my hand again, then released it suddenly. "T-bone! T-bone," I yelled. There was no response. A series of screams echoed the hallways of the hospital.

"Noooooooooooo!"

"My baby! Oh Lord, my baby!"

I grabbed my mother and held her tight, then broke away.

"Come back!" she yelled to me. "Please come back!"

I met my crew in the lounge area and told them we would meet in the spot in an hour.

When I got to the meeting spot and walked into the room, there was complete silence. I said, "I've never demanded anything of you or from you, but I want whoever done this—ASAP. Not next week, not two weeks from now, but right now."

Two days later, I got a phone call to meet at the spot in an hour. When I got there and went to the basement, I saw a guy hanging by his arms with blood all over him. Sed came over to me and said, "Take a deep breath. You will not believe this shit."

As I moved closer to get a better look at the

guy hanging there, my heart dropped and I yelled for everyone to leave the room.

"Art, you have to be shitting me! All I want to know is why!"

He said, "Brother, who the fuck you think you are talking to me like you did, flashing your money, acting like a little bitch not coming to see me while I was in jail.

I want you to feel the pain I had to go through. I've been on the grind ever since I got out, while you're over there being Mr. Superstar. You're living my life!"

"Art, you made the choice to stay in that car. You made the choice to smoke and drink. Everything that's happened to you is your fault—not mine. You almost killed my seed and you killed my brother—"

"Man," Art interrupted, "what, you thought you were just gonna get on your white horse and ride off into the sunset?"

"So you mean to tell me this is all because I decided to do good for myself!?"

There was a long pause. And then twelve shots rang out.

Seven years later, I was in a jail, wearing an orange jumpsuit with 201833 across my back, telling the end of my story. "What a difference a day makes. You can go from having everything to having nothing. You always have the last chance to choose right from wrong. It's your decision making that puts you in here, and you can't blame your parents or the place you live, and you can't blame the people around you. You have to take a look at yourself and see where you stand in this walk of life."

I peeled off the orange jumpsuit. Under it was my suit. "Now this is gangsta," I said with a smile, gesturing to my suit. "See, I chose to walk out of that basement seven years ago. I won a NCAA championship and played in the NBA until I blew out my knee. But most important, I graduated from college; I was the first in my family and neighborhood."

As I looked at the teenagers in their orange jumpsuits, I said, "I own two restaurants downtown, one night club, four massage parlors, and I'm the distributor of the construction helmets with the team logos on them. It's not over. You all made a mistake, but you can recover now. It's all on the decisions you make when you leave here. Remember, you can't blame anybody for how your life turns out. If you don't remember anything else I say, remember this—love yourself, and everything else will fall in place."

The crowd stood and cheered, and I made my way around the room greeting the teens. Afterwards, I went out to my car, and put my head back, and remembered it like it was yesterday …

I un-cocked my pistol and walked up out of the basement. I saw Sed go down the stairs and heard him say, "I never liked your punk ass anyway" before the shots rang out. I got in my car, looked out the window, and saw Sed walking out as the police pulled up. He smiled and winked at me and pointed his empty weapon.

About the Author

Amir Humphries was born on the Westside of Chicago in the early seventies, and grew up in the Abla Projects, located on S. Racine. There he shared a three bedroom apartment with his (late) Grandmother,(late) aunt, uncle, mother (sometimes) and two cousins. Amir was one of the fortunate kids from the projects, he attended a Catholic Pre-School in which he graduated kindergarten at the age of 4. At the age of eight Amir and his mother moved to Damen Courts. This was a whole new world to Amir. There he had carpet throughout the entire house, he had his own room and a color television. Life was looking good and going great. Then a new drug hit the streets called; CRACK COCAINE to which Amir's mother became a victim. With the exposure to the new drug on the street Amir learned about gangs and drugs at a early age by hanging with the older boys and seeing the dramatic changes his mother was going through. He later tried to play basketball which had its ups and downs because of the drastic change in his family situation his grades would fluctuate. Through out the violence he encountered, he was determined to stay focus and stay in school, after graduation at Crane High School he later joined the military. While serving he met the love of his life, had two beautiful kids, and a stepson. He now has four kids.

Amir is a great father and mentor; also coaches a High School Girls basketball team, and a AAU boys basketball team where he tries to instill the importance of making the right decisions and to today's youth.

Amir's purpose for this book is to inform the youth of today that the decisions you make while growing up can have a drastic effect on your life later on. By walking a way that night he is able to share this story with the youths of today. WHAT A DIFFERENCE A DAY MAKES!